A/79/49 (Vol. II)

Resolutions and Decisions
adopted by the General Assembly during its seventy-ninth session

Volume II

Decisions

10 September – 24 December 2024

General Assembly
Official Records • Seventy-ninth Session
Supplement No. 49

United Nations • New York, 2025

NOTE

The resolutions and decisions of the General Assembly are identified as follows:

Regular sessions

Until the thirtieth regular session, the resolutions of the General Assembly were identified by an arabic numeral followed by a roman numeral in parentheses indicating the session (for example: resolution 3363 (XXX)). When several resolutions were adopted under the same number, each of them was identified by a capital letter placed between the two numerals (for example: resolution 3367 A (XXX), resolutions 3411 A and B (XXX), resolutions 3419 A to D (XXX)). The decisions were not numbered.

Since the thirty-first session, as part of the new system adopted for symbols of General Assembly documents, resolutions and decisions have been identified by an arabic numeral, indicating the session, followed by an oblique stroke and another arabic numeral (for example: resolution 31/1, decision 31/301). When several resolutions or decisions were adopted under the same number, each of them has been identified by a capital letter placed after the two numerals (for example: resolution 31/16 A, resolutions 31/6 A and B, decisions 31/406 A to E).

Special sessions

Until the seventh special session, the resolutions of the General Assembly were identified by an arabic numeral followed, in parentheses, by the letter "S" and a roman numeral indicating the session (for example: resolution 3362 (S-VII)). The decisions were not numbered.

Since the eighth special session, resolutions and decisions have been identified by the letter "S" and an arabic numeral indicating the session, followed by an oblique stroke and another arabic numeral (for example: resolution S-8/1, decision S-8/11).

Emergency special sessions

Until the fifth emergency special session, the resolutions of the General Assembly were identified by an arabic numeral followed, in parentheses, by the letters "ES" and a roman numeral indicating the session (for example: resolution 2252 (ES-V)). The decisions were not numbered.

Since the sixth emergency special session, resolutions and decisions have been identified by the letters "ES" and an arabic numeral indicating the session, followed by an oblique stroke and another arabic numeral (for example: resolution ES-6/1, decision ES-6/11).

In each of the series described above, the numbering follows the order of adoption.

*

* *

The present volume contains the decisions adopted by the General Assembly from 10 September to 24 December 2024. Resolutions adopted by the Assembly during that period appear in volume I, together with information on the allocation of agenda items. Resolutions and decisions adopted subsequently during the seventy-ninth session will be published in volume III.

ISSN 0252-7014

Print ISBN: 978-92-1-003481-4

eISBN : 978-92-1-107166-5

Contents

Decisions

Page

A. Elections and appointments 4

B. Other decisions 9

1. Decisions adopted without reference to a Main Committee 9
2. Decisions adopted on the reports of the First Committee 24
3. Decisions adopted on the reports of the Special Political and Decolonization Committee (Fourth Committee) 27
4. Decisions adopted on the reports of the Second Committee 28
5. Decisions adopted on the reports of the Third Committee 31
6. Decisions adopted on the reports of the Fifth Committee 32
7. Decisions adopted on the reports of the Sixth Committee 34

Annex

Checklist of decisions 37

Decisions

Contents

Decision number	*Title*	*Page*
	A. Elections and appointments	
79/401.	Appointment of the members of the Credentials Committee	4
79/402.	Extension of the appointment of the Under-Secretary-General for Internal Oversight Services	4
79/403.	Election of members of the Human Rights Council	4
79/404.	Election of members of the Committee for Programme and Coordination	4
79/405.	Election of members of the Permanent Forum of People of African Descent	5
79/406.	Appointment of members of the Committee on Conferences	5
79/407.	Appointment of members of the Advisory Committee on Administrative and Budgetary Questions	5
79/408.	Appointment of members of the Committee on Contributions	6
79/409.	Confirmation of the appointment of members of the Investments Committee	6
79/410.	Appointment of members of the International Civil Service Commission	6
79/411.	Appointment of members and alternate members of the United Nations Staff Pension Committee	7
79/412.	Election of members of the United Nations Commission on International Trade Law	7
79/413.	Election of members of the Organizational Committee of the Peacebuilding Commission	8
	B. Other decisions	
	1. *Decisions adopted without reference to a Main Committee*	
79/501.	Meetings of subsidiary organs and entities during the main part of the seventy-ninth session	9
79/502.	General debate of the seventy-ninth session of the General Assembly	9
79/503.	Rights of reply to addresses by Heads of State	9
79/504.	Organization of the seventy-ninth session	9
79/505.	Adoption of the agenda and allocation of agenda items	10
79/506.	Summit of the Future	10
	Decision A	10
	Decision B	10
79/507.	Report of the International Residual Mechanism for Criminal Tribunals	11
79/508.	Report of the International Court of Justice	11
79/509.	Report of the Economic and Social Council	11
79/536.	Report of the Credentials Committee	11
79/537.	Further modalities of the Third United Nations Conference on Landlocked Developing Countries	11
	Decision A	11
	Decision B	12

Decision C ... 12

79/548. Participation of non-governmental organizations, civil society organizations, academic institutions and the private sector in the Fourth International Conference on Financing for Development ... 12

79/552. Agenda items remaining for consideration by the General Assembly at its seventy-ninth session ... 20

2. *Decisions adopted on the reports of the First Committee*

79/510. Reduction of military budgets ... 24

79/511. Maintenance of international security – good-neighbourliness, stability and development in South-Eastern Europe ... 25

79/512. Open-ended working group on the prevention of an arms race in outer space in all its aspects ... 25

79/513. Treaty banning the production of fissile material for nuclear weapons or other nuclear explosive devices ... 26

79/514. Missiles ... 26

79/515. Compliance with non-proliferation, arms limitation and disarmament agreements and commitments ... 26

79/516. Information on requests for votes ... 26

79/517. Provisional programme of work and timetable of the First Committee for 2025 ... 27

79/518. Programme planning (First Committee) ... 27

3. *Decisions adopted on the reports of the Special Political and Decolonization Committee (Fourth Committee)*

79/519. Increase in the membership of the Committee on the Peaceful Uses of Outer Space ... 27

Decision A ... 27

Decision B ... 27

79/520. Comprehensive review of the whole question of peacekeeping operations in all their aspects ... 28

79/521. Question of Gibraltar ... 28

79/522. Proposed programme of work and timetable of the Special Political and Decolonization Committee (Fourth Committee) for the eightieth session of the General Assembly ... 28

79/523. Programme planning (Special Political and Decolonization Committee (Fourth Committee)) ... 28

4. *Decisions adopted on the reports of the Second Committee*

79/542. Macroeconomic policy questions ... 28

79/543. Groups of countries in special situations ... 29

79/544. Operational activities for development ... 29

79/545. Draft programme of work of the Second Committee for the eightieth session of the General Assembly ... 29

79/546. Revitalization of the work of the Second Committee ... 30

79/547. Programme planning (Second Committee) ... 31

5. *Decisions adopted on the reports of the Third Committee*

79/538. Promotion and protection of human rights 31

79/539. Comprehensive implementation of and follow-up to the Vienna Declaration and Programme of Action 31

79/540. Draft programme of work of the Third Committee for the eightieth session of the General Assembly 31

79/541. Programme planning (Third Committee) 32

6. *Decisions adopted on the reports of the Fifth Committee*

79/549. Administrative and budgetary coordination of the United Nations with the specialized agencies and the International Atomic Energy Agency 32

79/550. Report on the activities of the Office of Internal Oversight Services 33

79/551. Questions deferred for future consideration 33

7. *Decisions adopted on the reports of the Sixth Committee*

79/524. Provisional programme of work of the Sixth Committee for the eightieth session 34

79/525. Programme planning (Sixth Committee) 35

79/526. Observer status for the Cooperation Council of Turkic-speaking States in the General Assembly 35

79/527. Observer status for the Eurasian Economic Union in the General Assembly 35

79/528. Observer status for the Community of Democracies in the General Assembly 35

79/529. Observer status for the Ramsar Convention on Wetlands Secretariat in the General Assembly 35

79/530. Observer status for the Global Environment Facility in the General Assembly 35

79/531. Observer status for the International Organization of Employers in the General Assembly 35

79/532. Observer status for the International Trade Union Confederation in the General Assembly 36

79/533. Observer status for the Boao Forum for Asia in the General Assembly 36

79/534. Observer status for the International Parliamentarians' Congress in the General Assembly 36

79/535. Observer status for the Regional Anti-Corruption Initiative in the General Assembly 36

A. Elections and appointments

79/401. Appointment of the members of the Credentials Committee

At its 1st plenary meeting, on 10 September 2024, the General Assembly, in accordance with rule 28 of its rules of procedure, appointed a Credentials Committee for its seventy-ninth session consisting of the following Member States: Antigua and Barbuda, Cabo Verde, China, Dominica, Lao People's Democratic Republic, Liberia, Monaco, Russian Federation and United States of America.

79/402. Extension of the appointment of the Under-Secretary-General for Internal Oversight Services

At its 2nd plenary meeting, on 13 September 2024, the General Assembly approved, notwithstanding resolution 48/218 B of 29 July 1994, the exceptional extension by the Secretary-General[1] of the term of Fatoumata Ndiaye (Senegal) as Under-Secretary-General for Internal Oversight Services by two years, until 24 October 2026.

79/403. Election of members of the Human Rights Council

At its 19th plenary meeting, on 9 October 2024, the General Assembly, pursuant to its resolutions 60/251 of 15 March 2006 and 65/281 of 17 June 2011, elected Benin, Bolivia (Plurinational State of), Colombia, Cyprus, Czechia, the Democratic Republic of the Congo, Ethiopia, the Gambia, Iceland, Kenya, the Marshall Islands, Mexico, North Macedonia, Qatar, the Republic of Korea, Spain, Switzerland and Thailand as members of the Human Rights Council for a three-year term of office beginning on 1 January 2025 to fill the vacancies occurring on the expiration of the terms of office of Argentina, Benin, Cameroon, Eritrea, Finland, the Gambia, Honduras, India, Kazakhstan, Lithuania, Luxembourg, Malaysia, Montenegro, Paraguay, Qatar, Somalia, the United Arab Emirates and the United States of America.

As a result, as of 1 January 2025, the Human Rights Council is composed of the following 47 Member States:[2] Albania,** Algeria,* Bangladesh,* Belgium,* Benin,*** Bolivia (Plurinational State of),*** Brazil,** Bulgaria,** Burundi,** Chile,* China,** Colombia,*** Costa Rica,* Côte d'Ivoire,** Cuba,** Cyprus,*** Czechia,*** Democratic Republic of the Congo,*** Dominican Republic,** Ethiopia,*** France,** Gambia,*** Georgia,* Germany,* Ghana,** Iceland,*** Indonesia,** Japan,** Kenya,*** Kuwait,** Kyrgyzstan,* Malawi,** Maldives,* Marshall Islands,*** Mexico,*** Morocco,* Netherlands (Kingdom of the),** North Macedonia,*** Qatar,*** Republic of Korea,*** Romania,* South Africa,* Spain,*** Sudan,* Switzerland,*** Thailand*** and Viet Nam.*

* Term of office expires on 31 December 2025.

** Term of office expires on 31 December 2026.

*** Term of office expires on 31 December 2027.

79/404. Election of members of the Committee for Programme and Coordination

At its 38th plenary meeting, on 13 November 2024, the General Assembly, on the basis of nominations by the Economic and Social Council[3] and in accordance with the annex to Council resolution 2008 (LX) of 14 May 1976 and Assembly decision 42/450 of 17 December 1987, elected Belgium, Botswana, France, Haiti, Kenya, Paraguay and the Russian Federation as members of the Committee for Programme and Coordination for a three-year term of office beginning on 1 January 2025 to fill the vacancies occurring on the expiration of the terms of office of Belgium, Botswana, Chile, France, Kenya, Paraguay and the Russian Federation.

As a result, as of 1 January 2025, the Committee for Programme and Coordination is composed of the following 34 Member States: Argentina,* Armenia,** Belgium,*** Botswana,*** Brazil,** Bulgaria,** Cameroon,** China,* Costa Rica,** Côte d'Ivoire,** France,*** Germany,** Haiti,*** India,** Iran (Islamic Republic of),** Israel,**

[1] See A/79/286.

[2] Benin, China, Côte d'Ivoire, Cuba, France, the Gambia, Germany, Malawi, Qatar and the Sudan are serving their second consecutive term.

[3] See A/79/522; see also Economic and Social Council decision 2024/204 B.

Italy,** Japan,** Kenya,*** Liberia,* Mexico,** Morocco,* Pakistan,** Paraguay,*** Philippines,* Poland,** Republic of Korea,* Russian Federation,*** Rwanda,** South Africa,** Tunisia,* United Kingdom of Great Britain and Northern Ireland,** United States of America** and Uruguay.**

---

* Term of office expires on 31 December 2025.

** Term of office expires on 31 December 2026.

*** Term of office expires on 31 December 2027.

79/405. Election of members of the Permanent Forum of People of African Descent

At its 38th plenary meeting, on 13 November 2024, the General Assembly, in accordance with its resolution 75/314 of 2 August 2021, elected the following persons as members of the Permanent Forum of People of African Descent for a three-year term of office beginning on 8 March 2025: Justin Hansford (United States of America), Martin Kimani (Kenya), Ana Janniel Matarrita McCalla (Costa Rica), Mona Omar (Egypt) and June Soomer (Saint Lucia).

79/406. Appointment of members of the Committee on Conferences

At its 38th plenary meeting, on 13 November 2024, the General Assembly, in accordance with paragraph 2 of its resolution 43/222 B of 21 December 1988, took note of the appointment by its President, after consultations with the Chairs of the regional groups concerned, of Brazil, the Congo, Hungary, Iran (Islamic Republic of), Mali, Paraguay and Portugal as members of the Committee on Conferences for a three-year term of office beginning on 1 January 2025.

As a result, as of 1 January 2025, the Committee on Conferences is composed of the following 21 Member States: Argentina,** Austria,* Botswana,** Brazil,*** China,* Congo,*** Djibouti,* Egypt,* France,** Guatemala,* Hungary,*** Iran (Islamic Republic of),*** Japan,* Mali,*** Paraguay,*** Philippines,** Portugal,*** Russian Federation,** Sierra Leone,** Sri Lanka** and United States of America.*

---

* Term of office expires on 31 December 2025.

** Term of office expires on 31 December 2026.

*** Term of office expires on 31 December 2027.

79/407. Appointment of members of the Advisory Committee on Administrative and Budgetary Questions

At its 38th plenary meeting, on 13 November 2024, the General Assembly, on the recommendation of the Fifth Committee,[4] appointed or reappointed the following persons as members of the Advisory Committee on Administrative and Budgetary Questions for a three-year term of office beginning on 1 January 2025: Amjad Qaid Al Kumaim (Yemen), Sharon Brennen-Haylock (Bahamas), Jakub Chmielewski (Poland), Paul Djoh Kpeye (Côte d'Ivoire) and Katlego Boase Mmalane (Botswana).

As a result, as of 1 January 2025, the Advisory Committee on Administrative and Budgetary Questions is composed as follows: Surendra Kumar Adhana (India),** Amjad Qaid Al Kumaim (Yemen),*** Abdallah Bachar Bong (Chad),** Feliksas Bakanauskas (Lithuania),** Ali Ben Said (Tunisia),** Sharon Brennen-Haylock (Bahamas),*** Jakub Chmielewski (Poland),*** Udo Klaus Fenchel (Germany),* Olivio Fermín (Dominican Republic),* Simon Horner (United Kingdom of Great Britain and Northern Ireland),** Carlo Jacobucci (Italy),* Ji Haojun (China),* Evgeny Kalugin (Russian Federation),** Paul Djoh Kpeye (Côte d'Ivoire),*** Julia Maciel (Paraguay),** Matsuda Yukiko (Japan),* Katlego Boase Mmalane (Botswana),*** Caroline Nalwanga (Uganda),** Juliana Gaspar Ruas (Brazil),** Stephani Laura Scheer (United States of America)** and Minhong Yi (Republic of Korea).*

---

* Term of office expires on 31 December 2025.

** Term of office expires on 31 December 2026.

*** Term of office expires on 31 December 2027.

---

[4] A/79/532, para. 4.

79/408. Appointment of members of the Committee on Contributions

At its 38th plenary meeting, on 13 November 2024, the General Assembly, on the recommendation of the Fifth Committee,[5] appointed or reappointed the following persons as members of the Committee on Contributions for a three-year term of office beginning on 1 January 2025: Syed Yawar Ali (Pakistan), Jasminka Dinić (Croatia), George Hannum (United States of America), Ihor Humennyi (Ukraine), René Michel Mizingou-Nzaba (Congo) and Suzuki Yoriko (Japan).

As a result, as of 1 January 2025, the Committee on Contributions is composed as follows: Syed Yawar Ali (Pakistan),*** Cheikh Tidiane Dème (Senegal),* Jasminka Dinić (Croatia),*** Gordon Eckersley (Australia),* Helena Concepción Felip Salazar (Paraguay),* Bernardo Greiver del Hoyo (Uruguay),* George Hannum (United States of America),*** Michael Holtsch (Germany),** Ihor Humennyi (Ukraine),*** Marcel Jullier (Switzerland),* Vadim Laputin (Russian Federation),** Lin Shan (China),** Joseph Masila (Kenya),* René Michel Mizingou-Nzaba (Congo),*** Hae-yun Park (Republic of Korea),** Henrique da Silveira Sardinha Pinto (Brazil),** Suzuki Yoriko (Japan)*** and Cihan Terzi (Türkiye).**

* Term of office expires on 31 December 2025.

** Term of office expires on 31 December 2026.

*** Term of office expires on 31 December 2027.

79/409. Confirmation of the appointment of members of the Investments Committee

At its 38th plenary meeting, on 13 November 2024, the General Assembly, on the recommendation of the Fifth Committee:[6]

(a) Confirmed the reappointment by the Secretary-General of Keiko Honda (Japan) as a regular member of the Investments Committee for a three-year term of office beginning on 1 January 2025;

(b) Confirmed the reappointment by the Secretary-General of Macky Tall (Mali) as an ad hoc member of the Investments Committee for a one-year term of office beginning on 1 January 2025.

As a result , as of 1 January 2025, the Investments Committee is composed as follows: Yasir O. Al-Rumayyan (Saudi Arabia, regular member),** Sarah Omotunde Alade (Nigeria, regular member),** Jens Fricke (Germany, regular member),* Keiko Honda (Japan, regular member),*** Natalia Khanjenkova (Russian Federation, regular member),** Michael Klein (United States of America, regular member),* Shan Li (China, regular member),** Patricia Parise (Argentina, regular member),** Luciane Ribeiro (Brazil, regular member)* and Macky Tall (Mali, ad hoc member).*

* Term of office expires on 31 December 2025.

** Term of office expires on 31 December 2026.

*** Term of office expires on 31 December 2027.

79/410. Appointment of members of the International Civil Service Commission

At its 38th plenary meeting, on 13 November 2024, the General Assembly, on the recommendation of the Fifth Committee,[7] appointed or reappointed the following persons as members of the International Civil Service Commission for a four-year term of office beginning on 1 January 2025: Larbi Djacta (Algeria), Andrei Ivanov (Russian Federation), Muhammad Abdul Muhith (Bangladesh), Sun Xudong (China) and El Hassane Zahid (Morocco).

As a result, as of 1 January 2025, the International Civil Service Commission is composed as follows: Larbi Djacta (Algeria)*** (Chair),** Boguslaw Winid (Poland)** (Vice-Chair),* Andrew Gbebay Bangali (Sierra Leone),**

[5] A/79/533, para. 4.

[6] A/79/534, para. 4.

[7] A/79/535, para. 6.

Xavier Bellmont Roldán (Spain),** Claudia Angélica Bueno Reynaga (Mexico),* Spyridon Flogaitis (Greece),* Andrei Ivanov (Russian Federation),*** Kaji Misako (Japan),* Ali Kurer (Libya),** Jeffrey Mounts (United States of America),* Muhammad Abdul Muhith (Bangladesh),*** Shauna Olney (Canada),* Sun Xudong (China),*** João Vargas (Brazil)** and El Hassane Zahid (Morocco).***

* Term of office expires on 31 December 2025.

** Term of office expires on 31 December 2026.

*** Term of office expires on 31 December 2028.

79/411. Appointment of members and alternate members of the United Nations Staff Pension Committee

At its 38th plenary meeting, on 13 November 2024, the General Assembly, on the recommendation of the Fifth Committee,[8] appointed or reappointed the following persons as members or alternate members of the United Nations Staff Pension Committee for a four-year term of office beginning on 1 January 2025: Dmitry S. Chumakov (Russian Federation), Kozaki Hitoshi (Japan), Lovemore Mazemo (Zimbabwe), Philip Richard Okanda Owade (Kenya), Mustafizur Rahman (Bangladesh), Jörg Stosberg (Germany) and David Traystman (United States of America).

At its 48th plenary meeting, on 6 December 2024, the General Assembly, on the recommendation of the Fifth Committee,[9] appointed Guillermo Rodolico (Argentina) as a member or alternate member of the United Nations Staff Pension Committee for a four-year term of office beginning on 1 January 2025.

As a result, as of 1 January 2025, the members and alternate members of the United Nations Staff Pension Committee appointed by the General Assembly are as follows: Dmitry S. Chumakov (Russian Federation), Kozaki Hitoshi (Japan), Lovemore Mazemo (Zimbabwe), Philip Richard Okanda Owade (Kenya), Mustafizur Rahman (Bangladesh), Guillermo Rodolico (Argentina), Jörg Stosberg (Germany) and David Traystman (United States of America).

79/412. Election of members of the United Nations Commission on International Trade Law

At its 40th plenary meeting, on 20 November 2024, the General Assembly, in accordance with section II, paragraphs 1 to 3, of its resolution 2205 (XXI) of 17 December 1966, as amended by paragraph 8 of its resolution 3108 (XXVIII) of 12 December 1973 and paragraph 10 (b) of its resolution 31/99 of 15 December 1976, as well as its resolutions 57/20 of 19 November 2002 and 76/109 of 9 December 2021, elected Belgium, Bolivia (Plurinational State of), Burundi, Canada, China, the Congo, Côte d'Ivoire, the Dominican Republic, El Salvador, France, Germany, Ghana, Hungary, Japan, Malaysia, Mauritania, Mexico, Peru, the Philippines, the Republic of Korea, the Russian Federation, Sierra Leone, Singapore, South Africa, Sri Lanka, Sweden, Switzerland, the United Kingdom of Great Britain and Northern Ireland, Uruguay, Viet Nam and Zambia as members of the United Nations Commission on International Trade Law for a six-year term of office beginning on 7 July 2025 and expiring on the last day prior to the beginning of the sixty-fourth session of the Commission, in 2031, to fill the vacancies occurring on the expiration of the terms of office of Algeria, Belgium, Cameroon, Canada, China, Côte d'Ivoire, Croatia, the Dominican Republic, Ecuador, Finland, France, Germany, Ghana, Honduras, Hungary, Indonesia, Japan, Malaysia, Mali, Mexico, Peru, the Republic of Korea, the Russian Federation, Singapore, South Africa, Switzerland, Ukraine, the United Kingdom of Great Britain and Northern Ireland, Viet Nam and Zimbabwe and 5 of the 10 additional seats stipulated in resolution 76/109.

As a result, as of 7 July 2025, the United Nations Commission on International Trade Law is composed of the following 66 Member States:[10] Afghanistan,* Argentina,* Armenia,* Australia,* Austria,* Belarus,* Belgium,** Bolivia (Plurinational State of),** Brazil,* Bulgaria,* Burundi,** Canada,** Chile,* China,** Congo,** Côte d'Ivoire,** Colombia,* Czechia,* Democratic Republic of the Congo,* Dominican Republic,** El Salvador,** France,** Germany,** Ghana,** Greece,* Hungary,** India,* Iran (Islamic Republic of),* Iraq,* Israel,* Italy,*

[8] A/79/536, para. 4.

[9] A/79/536/Add.1, para. 4.

[10] Three vacancies for members from Eastern European States and one vacancy for a member from Western European and other States remain to be filled for a six-year term of office beginning on 7 July 2025 and expiring on the last day prior to the beginning of the sixty-fourth session of the Commission, in 2031.

Japan,** Kenya,* Kuwait,* Malawi,* Malaysia,** Mauritania,** Mauritius,* Mexico,** Morocco,* Nigeria,* Panama,* Peru,** Philippines,** Poland,* Republic of Korea,** Russian Federation,** Saudi Arabia,* Sierra Leone,** Singapore,** Somalia,* South Africa,** Spain,* Sri Lanka,** Sweden,** Switzerland,** Thailand,* Türkiye,* Turkmenistan,* Uganda,* United Kingdom of Great Britain and Northern Ireland,** United States of America,* Uruguay,** Venezuela (Bolivarian Republic of),* Viet Nam** and Zambia.**

---

* Term of office expires on the last day prior to the beginning of the sixty-first session of the Commission, in 2028.

** Term of office expires on the last day prior to the beginning of the sixty-fourth session of the Commission, in 2031.

79/413. Election of members of the Organizational Committee of the Peacebuilding Commission

At its 54th plenary meeting, on 19 December 2024, the General Assembly, pursuant to its resolutions 60/180 of 20 December 2005, 60/261 of 8 May 2006 and 63/145 of 18 December 2008, elected Brazil, Cambodia, Egypt, Morocco and Uganda as members of the Organizational Committee of the Peacebuilding Commission for a two-year term of office beginning on 1 January 2025 to fill the vacancies occurring on the expiration of the terms of office of Egypt, Kenya, Qatar, Saint Vincent and the Grenadines and South Africa.

Pursuant to paragraphs 4 (a) to (d) of resolution 60/180, 25 States have already been elected and/or selected as members of the Organizational Committee of the Peacebuilding Commission: Poland and Uruguay elected by the General Assembly;[11] Algeria, China, France, Panama, Russian Federation, United Kingdom of Great Britain and Northern Ireland and United States of America selected by the Security Council;[12] Australia, Colombia, Kenya, Netherlands (Kingdom of the), Republic of Korea and South Africa elected by the Economic and Social Council;[13] Canada, Germany, Japan, Norway and Sweden selected by and from among the top 10 providers of assessed contributions to United Nations budgets and of voluntary contributions to United Nations funds, programmes and agencies, including a standing peacebuilding fund;[14] and Bangladesh, India, Nepal, Pakistan and Rwanda selected by and from among the top 10 providers of military personnel and civilian police to United Nations missions.[15]

As a result, on 1 January 2025, the Organizational Committee of the Peacebuilding Commission is composed of the following 30 Member States:[16] Algeria,** Australia,**** Bangladesh,*** Brazil,*** Cambodia,*** Canada,*** China,* Colombia,**** Egypt,*** France,* Germany,*** India,*** Japan,*** Kenya,**** Morocco,*** Nepal,*** Netherlands (Kingdom of the),**** Norway,*** Pakistan,*** Panama,** Poland,** Republic of Korea,**** Russian Federation,* Rwanda,*** South Africa,**** Sweden,*** Uganda,*** United Kingdom of Great Britain and Northern Ireland,* United States of America* and Uruguay.**

---

* Permanent members of the Security Council.

** Term of office expires on 31 December 2025.

*** Term of office expires on 31 December 2026.

**** Term of office expires on 31 December 2026 or when they cease to be members of the Economic and Social Council, whichever comes earlier.

---

[11] See decision 78/411.

[12] See S/2025/13.

[13] See Economic and Social Council decisions 2024/220 A and B and 2025/209.

[14] See A/79/672.

[15] See A/79/630.

[16] One vacancy for a member from Eastern European States to be elected by the Economic and Social Council remains to be filled for a term of office beginning on the date of election and ending on 31 December 2026 or when it ceases to be a member of the Council, whichever comes earlier.

B. Other decisions

1. *Decisions adopted without reference to a Main Committee*

79/501. Meetings of subsidiary organs and entities during the main part of the seventy-ninth session

At its 1st plenary meeting, on 10 September 2024, the General Assembly decided to authorize those entities listed in the letter dated 3 September 2024 from the Chair of the Committee on Conferences,[17] namely the Committee on the Exercise of the Inalienable Rights of the Palestinian People, the Executive Board of the United Nations Entity for Gender Equality and the Empowerment of Women, the Group of Governmental Experts on the continuing operation of the United Nations Register of Conventional Arms, the Conference on the Establishment of a Middle East Zone Free of Nuclear Weapons and Other Weapons of Mass Destruction, the Committee on Relations with the Host Country, the open-ended working group on security of and in the use of information and communications technologies 2021–2025, the Independent Audit Advisory Committee, the Working Group of the Whole of the Special Committee on Peacekeeping Operations, and the Meeting of States Parties to the United Nations Convention on the Law of the Sea, to meet during the main part of the seventy-ninth session of the General Assembly, on the strict understanding that all such meetings would be allocated conference services in such a way as to ensure that the work of the General Assembly and its Main Committees is not impeded.

79/502. General debate of the seventy-ninth session of the General Assembly

At its 2nd plenary meeting, on 13 September 2024, the General Assembly, on the recommendation of the General Committee as set forth in its first report,[18] and taking note that, pursuant to resolution 57/301 of 13 March 2003, the general debate would begin at 9 a.m. on Tuesday, 24 September 2024, and would continue on Wednesday, Thursday and Friday, 25–27 September, and on Monday, 30 September, decided that the general debate would continue on Saturday, 28 September 2024, in order to maximize the number of speakers during that week..

79/503. Rights of reply to addresses by Heads of State

At its 2nd plenary meeting, on 13 September 2024, the General Assembly took note of the information provided in paragraph 53 of the report of the General Committee[19] concerning rights of reply to addresses by Heads of State.

79/504. Organization of the seventy-ninth session

At its 2nd plenary meeting, on 13 September 2024, the General Assembly, on the recommendation of the General Committee as set forth in its first report,[20] adopted a number of provisions concerning the organization of the seventy-ninth session.

At its 42nd plenary meeting, on 26 November 2024, the General Assembly, on the proposal of its President, decided to postpone the date of recess of the seventy-ninth session of the Assembly from Monday, 9 December 2024, to Thursday, 19 December 2024.

At the same meeting, the General Assembly, at the request of the Chair of the Fifth Committee, decided to extend the work of the Committee until Friday, 13 December 2024.

At its 52nd plenary meeting, on 12 December 2024, the General Assembly, on the proposal of its President, decided to further postpone the date of recess of the seventy-ninth session of the Assembly from Thursday, 19 December 2024 to Monday, 23 December 2024.

At the same meeting, the General Assembly, at the request of the Chair of the Fifth Committee, decided to further extend the work of the Committee until Friday, 20 December 2024.

[17] A/79/335.

[18] A/79/250, para. 37.

[19] A/79/250.

[20] A/79/250.

79/505. Adoption of the agenda and allocation of agenda items

At its 2nd plenary meeting, on 13 September 2024, the General Assembly, on the recommendation of the General Committee as set forth in its first report,[21] adopted the agenda[22] and the allocation of agenda items[23] for the seventy-ninth session.

At the same meeting, the General Assembly, on the recommendation of the General Committee as set forth in its first report,[24] decided to include in the agenda of its seventy-ninth session the item entitled "Question of the Comorian island of Mayotte", under heading B (Maintenance of international peace and security), on the understanding that there would be no consideration of this item by the Assembly.

Also at the same meeting, the General Assembly, on the recommendation of the General Committee as set forth in its first report,[25] decided to defer consideration of the item entitled "Question of the Malagasy islands of Glorieuses, Juan de Nova, Europa and Bassas da India" and to include it in the provisional agenda of its eightieth session.

At its 54th plenary meeting, on 19 December 2024, the General Assembly, on the proposal of the Secretary-General,[26] having waived the relevant provisions of rule 40 of its rules of procedure, decided to include in the agenda of its seventy-ninth session an additional sub-item entitled "Appointment of members of the Independent Audit Advisory Committee", as sub-item (l) of agenda item 116 entitled "Appointments to fill vacancies in subsidiary organs and other appointments" under heading I (Organizational, administrative and other matters), and to allocate it to the Fifth Committee.

At the same meeting, the General Assembly decided to consider directly in plenary meeting agenda item 17 entitled "Follow-up to and implementation of the outcomes of the International Conferences on Financing for Development", under heading A (Promotion of sustained economic growth and sustainable development in accordance with the relevant resolutions of the General Assembly and recent United Nations conferences), and to proceed expeditiously with the consideration of a draft decision[27] and a draft amendment thereto.[28]

Also at the same meeting, the General Assembly decided to consider directly in plenary meeting sub-item (a) entitled "Role of the United Nations in promoting development in the context of globalization and interdependence" of agenda item 20 entitled "Globalization and interdependence", under heading A (Promotion of sustained economic growth and sustainable development in accordance with the relevant resolutions of the General Assembly and recent United Nations conferences), and to proceed expeditiously with the consideration of a draft resolution.[29]

79/506. Summit of the Future

A

At its 3rd plenary meeting, on 22 September 2024, the General Assembly decided that, after the departure of the Secretary-General, his seat at the podium might be occupied by his representative.

B

At its 3rd plenary meeting, on 22 September 2024, the General Assembly decided to reopen the list of speakers for three additional delegations to hear their statements at the last position in the appropriate category at the 4th plenary meeting, on 22 September 2024.

---

[21] A/79/250.

[22] A/79/251.

[23] A/79/252.

[24] A/79/250, para. 94.

[25] Ibid., para. 95.

[26] A/79/638.

[27] A/79/L.44.

[28] A/79/L.50.

[29] A/79/L.46.

79/507. Report of the International Residual Mechanism for Criminal Tribunals

At its 23rd plenary meeting, on 16 October 2024, the General Assembly took note of the twelfth annual report of the International Residual Mechanism for Criminal Tribunals.[30]

79/508. Report of the International Court of Justice

At its 31st plenary meeting, on 30 October 2024, the General Assembly took note of the report of the International Court of Justice.[31]

79/509. Report of the Economic and Social Council

At its 34th plenary meeting, on 5 November 2024, the General Assembly took note of the report of the Economic and Social Council.[32]

79/536. Report of the Credentials Committee

At its 48th plenary meeting, on 6 December 2024, the General Assembly decided to accept the information concerning the appointment of representatives of Sierra Leone to the seventy-ninth session of the Assembly.

79/537. Further modalities of the Third United Nations Conference on Landlocked Developing Countries

A

At its 48th plenary meeting, on 6 December 2024, the General Assembly, on the proposal of Bhutan, Bolivia (Plurinational State of), Botswana, Burkina Faso, the Central African Republic, the Congo, Eswatini, Kazakhstan, Kyrgyzstan, the Lao People's Democratic Republic, Lesotho, Malawi, Mali, Mongolia, Morocco, Nepal, the Niger, Paraguay, the Republic of Moldova, Rwanda, Serbia, Tajikistan, Turkmenistan, Uganda, the United Republic of Tanzania and Zimbabwe,[33] recalling its resolutions 76/217 of 17 December 2021, 77/246 of 30 December 2022 and 77/329 of 25 August 2023, in which the Assembly had decided to convene the Third United Nations Conference on Landlocked Developing Countries at the highest possible level, including Heads of State and Government, recalling also its decision 78/550 of 7 May 2024 and its resolution 78/315 of 10 July 2024, by which it had decided to hold the Conference in Gaborone from 10 to 13 December 2024, and noting that the Conference would not be held, as planned, from 10 to 13 December 2024, decided:

(a) That the Third United Nations Conference on Landlocked Developing Countries shall be postponed to a later date and shall be held at a venue to be decided;

(b) On an exceptional basis, to convene a meeting of the General Assembly in December 2024 to consider the draft new Programme of Action for Landlocked Developing Countries for the Decade 2024–2034[34] and that the meeting would hear statements by the President of the General Assembly, the Chair of the Group of Landlocked Developing Countries and the Secretary-General of the Third United Nations Conference on Landlocked Developing Countries, to be followed by the adoption of the draft Programme of Action;

(c) To request the Secretary-General of the Third United Nations Conference on Landlocked Developing Countries to conduct further consultations on the next steps, including identifying the dates and venue of the Conference.

---

[30] A/79/249-S/2024/570.

[31] *Official Records of the General Assembly, Seventy-ninth Session, Supplement No. 4* (A/79/4).

[32] *Official Records of the General Assembly, Seventy-ninth Session, Supplement No. 3* (A/79/3).

[33] A/79/L.20.

[34] A/79/L.21.

B

At its 55th (resumed) plenary meeting, on 24 December 2024, the General Assembly, under rule 81 of its rules of procedure, decided to reconsider the provision contained in paragraph (b) of decision 79/537 A of 6 December 2024.

C

At its 55th (resumed) plenary meeting, on 24 December 2024, the General Assembly decided to proceed to take action on draft resolution A/79/L.21 while hearing in January 2025 the statements mandated in its decision 79/537 A of 6 December 2024 and any statements in explanation of vote on the draft resolution.

79/548. Participation of non-governmental organizations, civil society organizations, academic institutions and the private sector in the Fourth International Conference on Financing for Development

At its 54th plenary meeting, on 19 December 2024, the General Assembly, on the proposal of its President,[35] as amended,[36] recalling paragraph 4 (b) of its resolution 78/271 of 11 April 2024, entitled "Further modalities of the Fourth International Conference on Financing for Development", decided to approve the participation of the non-governmental organizations, civil society organizations, academic institutions and the private sector as listed in the annex to the present decision in the Fourth International Conference on Financing for Development and its preparatory process, to be held pursuant to resolutions 78/271, and 78/231 of 22 December 2023.

Annex

ACM - Association for Computing Machinery

Advancement of Rural Kids

Africa Sustainable Climate and Environment Foundation LBG

Africa-Europe Foundation

AfroLeadership

Alianza por los Derechos, la Igualdad y la Solidaridad Internacional

Alive Today

All in foundation (AIF)

All Nations Arise and Manifest Initiative for the Less Privileged (ANAM Initiative)

All-Africa Students Union

Alliance for Development

Alsaid Foundation

AMBASSADEURS DE L'ENVIRONNEMENT (ADE)

American Football For African Mission

Angel Wisdom Investment Co., Ltd

Anthropocene Fixed Income Institute

APCO Worldwide LLC

Asociación Iniciativa Retorno por el Desarrollo de África Subsahariana. (IRDAS)

Asociación Instituto ipades para la Promoción de la Paz y el Desarrollo

---

[35] A/79/L.44.

[36] A/79/L.50.

Asociación Mexicana de Neuroética

Asociación para el Cambio Social, AXC

Associação para Integridade de Crianças e Jovens em Angola (AICJA)

Association alfarah de devlopment

Association Congolaise pour le Développement Agricole ACDA FRANCE

ASSOCIATION DES JEUNES AGRICULTEURS DU MALI (AJAM)

ASSOCIATION DES PERSONNES PATRIOTES DU BURUNDI (APPBU)

ASSOCIATION POUR LE DEVELOPPEMENT AGROPASTORAL, L'ENVIRONNEMENT ET LA CULTURE

Association pour le Développement Socio-Economique et Technologique de la Jeunesse (ONG ADEJ-Mali)

Association SIRABA SCHOOL

Asuntos del Sur

Ayuda en Accion

Bagmati UNESCO Club

BARWAQA RELIEF ORGANIZATION

Bell And Bridge Crystal Foundation

BERINE AND BOKWE FOUNDATION

BIECE-AE

Boston Consulting Group

Bread for the World Institute

BREAD OF PEACE

Bridging Gaps Microloans gUG

CADIRE CAMEROON ASSOCIATION

Capital for Climate

CEE Bankwatch Network

CELIOS Pencerah Bangsa Foundation

Center for Climate and Sustainability empowerment

Center for Fiscal Transparency and Public Integrity

Center for International Private Enterprise

Centre for Drinking Water Agriculture Development and Environment Improvement CDADEI

Centre for Feminist Foreign Policy (CFFP)

Centre for Peace and Development Initiatives (CPDI)

Charles Stewart Mott Foundation

Chemichemi Foundation

Children's Investment Fund Foundation

Christian Care Foundation Pakistan

Civil Power Development Center

Clean Climate And Environment Campaign Initiative

Climate Justice Programme

Climate Vulnerable Forum Lbg

ClimateWorks Foundation

Coalition Climat pour la Biodiversité et le Développement (CCBD-Congo)

CommUnity of the Deaf, Inc

Coordinadora Andaluza de ONGD (CAONGD)

CRPM Skopje

DAI Global UK

Dalberg Catalyst

Danish Family Planning Association, Sex & Samfund

Danish Institute for International Studies

DEBT JUSTICE NORGE

Deloitte Climate & Sustainability S.r.l. S.B.

DYNAMIQUE DES FEMMES POUR LA REFORME DE L'ADMINISTRATION PUBLIQUE

EAGLE WOMEN EMPOWERMENT CLUB

EDUCO

Eductrade S.A.

Emonyo Yefwe International

Empowered Women and Youth Globally

Equidad de Género, Ciudadanía, Trabajo y Familia, A.C.

Erste Asset Management GmbH

ESS Forum International/Rencontres du Mont Blanc

European Development Finance Institutions (EDFI)

Family organization for empowerment FOREM

FAWAN ACTION NETWORK (Women Environmental Network)

Fern

FMO

FOGGS - Foundation for Global Governance and Sustainability

Fondo Centroamericano de Mujeres

Forum of Federations

Fundacion ADES - Asesores en Desarrollo Social -

Fundación Entreculturas - Fe y Alegría

Fundación Mundubat

Fundacion Real Instituto Elcano de Estudios Internacionales y Estratégicos

Fundacion Save the Children

Fundación UNICEF Comité Español

Fundar Centro de Analisis e Investigacion

Generation Without Qat Organization

Ghana Integrity Initiative

Ghana Russia Center for Commerce and Relations

Girls Aid Movement

GiveDirectly

GK Partners

Global AI

Global Center on Adaptation

Global Governance Forum

Global Impact

Global Marshall Plan Foundation

Global Student Forum/Globale Studerende Danmark

Global Surgery Umbrella

Global Women Leadership Foundation

GLOBART

Grupo de Cambio Climático para Latinoamérica y el Caribe

GWL Voices

GYAN GHANA

Hablemos CO

Healthy Community Foundation

Helping Hearts Foundation

Her Dream Initiative for Women and the Girl Child

HIRED Consult

HOMECOMING SENEGAMBIE

Human Rights and Environment Improvement Center HREIC

Humanitaire Sans Frontière

Humanitarian Action for Africa

Humanitarian Journalism and Media Interventions (HumanizaCom)

Humanitarian Organization for Poverty Eradication – Pakistan

I4CE - Institute for Climate Economics

Impact Compact LLC

Inclusive Society Institute

Institut Méditerranéen de l’Eau

Institute for Environment and Development Europe (IIED Europe)

Institute for Global Negotiation

Intergenerational Center for Global Action

International Commission of Culture and Diplomatic Relations

International Council for Adult Education (ICAE)

International Fund for Public Interest Media

International Treatment Preparedness Coalition

Investhill Group

Irish Development Education Association (IDEA)

ISC Intelligence in Science

JANAHIT GRAMIN SEWA SAMITI

Joep Lange Institute Center for Global Health Diplomacy

Journalists' Environmental Association of Tanzania

Jubilee USA Network

JUSTA | Associação Plataformas - Ideias e Projetos para Soluções Públicas

Kamana Health Nepal

Kelechi Okwaraji Mental health foundation

Kelem Ethiopia

KIWONNONGO FOUNDATION

Klimadelegation e.V.

KONATE business

La Coordinadora de Organizaciones para el Desarrollo

Lafede – Organitzacions per a la Justicia Global

Latin American Health Organization / Corporación Latinoamericana para la Salud

LEADERS DE DEMAIN

Leadership Development Association International

Les Eaux Minérales d'Oulmès

Levoca LLC

Lowy Institute

M.Sethia & Co.

McMaster University

Meridian Institute

Microsoft Corporation

Migration Youth and Children Platform CIC

Mission Foundation Movement

MORNINGSTAR Sustainalytics

Muhammad Akram Sons Trading Investment

Munich Climate Insurance Initiative

National Democratic Institute for International Affairs

National Senior citizens Organization of Liberia

NCD Alliance

New World Hope Organization (NWHO)

NGO OADES-Niger

Norwegian Church Aid

Nuveen

Oil Change International

One Africa Trust

Open Capital Advisors Limited

Open Contracting Partnership

Organisation de Développement des Recherches Agricole et la Protection de la Nature

Organisation pour la lutte contre les Stupéfiants, Boissons Prohibées, Tabagisme et Alcoolisme (OLCOS)

Oxfam Intermón

Pan African Chamber of Culture, Trade and Investment LTD/GTE

Pan African Health Professionals Organisation - PAHPO

Partenariat France et Afrique pour le co développement (PFAC)

Peoples Development Community (PDC)

PGIM Quantitative Solutions

PharmAccess

Plan International Ireland

Plant for planet Côte d'Ivoire

Plataforma CIPÓ

Poverty Eradication and Sustainable Action Aid (PESAID)

PRI Association

Pro Natura - Friends of the Earth Switzerland

Professionals For Humanity Initiative (PROFOH)

Programme de Developpement Humaniatire et Logistique PDHL

Prospective Generation Foundation

Proteus Fund

Rainforest Action Network

REACHOUT SALONE

Reality of Aid - Asia Pacific

Refugee Talent Group RTG

Res Non Verba- Civic House

Rescue Mission International (ReMI)

Reseau des Organisations des Jeunes Africains Leaders des Nations Unies (ROJALNU Burkina Faso)

Resilient40

Right to Education Initiative

Rural Community Development Program Nepal

Rural Mutual Development, Dhading

Saint Louis University, Madrid, Spain.

School of Economics and Business Norwegian University of Life Sciences (NMBU), Skatteforsk - Centre for Tax Research

School of International Futures

SEB Investment Management AB

SEDRA-FEDERACIÓN PLANIFICACIÓN FAMILIAR

Shamba Centre for Food & Climate

She Forum Africa Initiative

Shenzhen GLAT Fund Investment Management CO., Ltd

Sinergia Animal

Society of Gender Professionals

Somali Weyn Development Organization (SOWDO)

Soulbeegood

Soutien Social

Sport For Change

Standard Chartered PLC

Stichting Circle Economy

Stichting European Climate Foundation

Stichting Re-course International

Stichting Youth for Sustainable Travel

Strategia Development Research Institute

Student Business Organization for Sustainable Development (SBOSD Ghana)

Sustainable Energy and Enterprise Development for Communities, Inc.

SUSTAINABLE ENVIRONMENT FOOD AND AGRICULTURE INITIATIVE

Sustainable Organization for Rural Development (SORD)

Swedish Migration & Refugees Assistance

Taha Enterprise

Tanzania Trade and Investment Coalition (TATIC)

Tax Justice Norway

The Brookings Institution

The Institute for Fiscal Studies

The Iraqi Institution for Development

The Millennials Movement

The Private Infrastructure Development Group

The Soil Solution

The Special Physically Challenged Care Foundation

Theodora Anavhe Adamu Foundation (TAAF)

Therismos Initiative for Development and Empowerment

Third Generation Environmentalism Ltd

TONGZHOU CLUB (BEIJING) INFORMATION TECHNOLOGY CO., LTD

Toronto Leadership Centre

Transat Ventures Lab

UNCAC Coalition

United Nations Association of Africa, UNAA, USA, INC.

Universidad Complutense de Madrid

Universidad de Sevilla, Facultad de Derecho

University of Antwerp

University of Barcelona

University of British Columbia Centre for Climate Justice

University Of Ghana

University of Warwick

Urgewald

Velliv, Pension & Livsforsikring A/S

Venezolanos en Barranquilla

Vested Impact Ltd

Village Farmers Initiative (VFI)

WAMECCH CBO

Water For People

We Belong Here INC.

We The World Botswana Chapter

Women and Youth Advancement Inc.

World Economic Forum

World Humanitarian Forum

WWF Spain

Youth and Women for Peace and Sustainable Development

Youth awareness and development organization

Youth Finance for Good

Youth for Tax Justice Network

Youthinkgreen - jugend denkt um.welt

Zhongtai Jiye Investment Group Co., Ltd

79/552. Agenda items remaining for consideration by the General Assembly at its seventy-ninth session

At its 55th (resumed) plenary meeting, on 24 December 2024, the General Assembly, apart from organizational matters, took note of the following agenda items that remained for consideration during its seventy-ninth session:

Item 9. Report of the Economic and Social Council

Item 11. Implementation of the Declaration of Commitment on HIV/AIDS and the political declarations on HIV/AIDS

Item 12. Sport for development and peace

Item 13. Integrated and coordinated implementation of and follow-up to the outcomes of the major United Nations conferences and summits in the economic, social and related fields

Item 14. Culture of peace

Item 17. Follow-up to and implementation of the outcomes of the International Conferences on Financing for Development.

Item 18. Sustainable development

Item 21. Groups of countries in special situations:

(b) Follow-up to the third United Nations Conference on Landlocked Developing Countries

Item 28. Report of the Security Council

Item 29. Report of the Peacebuilding Commission

Item 30. Elimination of unilateral extraterritorial coercive economic measures as a means of political and economic compulsion

Item 31. The role of diamonds in fuelling conflict

Item 32. Prevention of armed conflict:

(a) Prevention of armed conflict

(b) Strengthening the role of mediation in the peaceful settlement of disputes, conflict prevention and resolution

Item 33. Protracted conflicts in the GUAM area and their implications for international peace, security and development

Item 34. The situation in the Middle East

Item 35. Question of Palestine

Item 36. The situation in Afghanistan

Item 37. Question of the Comorian island of Mayotte

Item 39. The situation in Central America: progress in fashioning a region of peace, freedom, democracy and development

Item 40. Question of Cyprus

Item 41. Armed aggression against the Democratic Republic of the Congo

Item 42. Question of the Falkland Islands (Malvinas)

Item 43. The situation of democracy and human rights in Haiti

Item 44. Armed Israeli aggression against the Iraqi nuclear installations and its grave consequences for the established international system concerning the peaceful uses of nuclear energy, the non-proliferation of nuclear weapons and international peace and security

Item 45. Consequences of the Iraqi occupation of and aggression against Kuwait

Item 51. Comprehensive review of the whole question of peacekeeping operations in all their aspects

Item 61. Peacebuilding and sustaining peace

Item 62. The situation in the temporarily occupied territories of Ukraine

Item 63. Use of the veto

Item 64. Zone of peace, trust and cooperation of Central Asia

Item 65. From the New Partnership for Africa's Development to Agenda 2063: progress in the implementation of sustainable development in Africa and international support:

(a) From the New Partnership for Africa's Development to Agenda 2063: progress in the implementation of sustainable development in Africa and international support

(b) Causes of conflict and the promotion of durable peace and sustainable development in Africa

Item 69. Elimination of racism, racial discrimination, xenophobia and related intolerance

Item 72. Strengthening of the coordination of humanitarian and disaster relief assistance of the United Nations, including special economic assistance:

(a) Strengthening of the coordination of emergency humanitarian assistance of the United Nations

(b) Assistance to the Palestinian people

(c) Special economic assistance to individual countries or regions

Item 73. Report of the International Court of Justice

Item 75. Oceans and the law of the sea:

(a) Oceans and the law of the sea

(c) Agreement under the United Nations Convention on the Law of the Sea on the Conservation and Sustainable Use of Marine Biological Diversity of Areas beyond National Jurisdiction

Item 87. Request for an advisory opinion of the International Court of Justice on the legal consequences of the separation of the Chagos Archipelago from Mauritius in 1965

Item 88. Extraordinary Chambers in the Courts of Cambodia – residual functions

Item 98. General and complete disarmament

Item 111. Report of the Secretary-General on the work of the Organization

Item 112. Report of the Secretary-General on the Peacebuilding Fund

Item 113. Notification by the Secretary-General under Article 12, paragraph 2, of the Charter of the United Nations

Item 114. Elections to fill vacancies in principal organs:

(a) Election of non-permanent members of the Security Council

(b) Election of members of the Economic and Social Council

Item 115. Elections to fill vacancies in subsidiary organs and other elections:

(d) Election of members of the United Nations Commission on International Trade Law

Item 116. Appointments to fill vacancies in subsidiary organs and other appointments:

(g) Confirmation of the appointment of the Administrator of the United Nations Development Programme

(h) Confirmation of the appointment of the Secretary-General of the United Nations Conference on Trade and Development

(i) Appointment of members of the Joint Inspection Unit

(k) Appointment of members of the Board of the 10-Year Framework of Programmes on Sustainable Consumption and Production Patterns

(l) Appointment of members of the Independent Audit Advisory Committee

Item 117. Admission of new Members to the United Nations

Item 118. Follow-up to the outcome of the Millennium Summit

Item 119. Commemoration of the abolition of slavery and the transatlantic slave trade

Item 120. Implementation of the resolutions of the United Nations

Item 121. Revitalization of the work of the General Assembly

Item 122. Question of equitable representation on and increase in the membership of the Security Council and other matters related to the Security Council

Item 123. Strengthening of the United Nations system:

(a) Strengthening of the United Nations system

(b) Central role of the United Nations system in global governance

Item 124. United Nations reform: measures and proposals

Item 125. Cooperation between the United Nations and regional and other organizations:

(a) Cooperation between the United Nations and the African Union

(c) Cooperation between the United Nations and the Asian-African Legal Consultative Organization

(f) Cooperation between the United Nations and the Organization of American States

(g) Cooperation between the United Nations and the Organization for Security and Cooperation in Europe

(h) Cooperation between the United Nations and the Caribbean Community

(i) Cooperation between the United Nations and the Economic Cooperation Organization

(j) Cooperation between the United Nations and the International Organization of la Francophonie

(l) Cooperation between the United Nations and the Council of Europe

(m) Cooperation between the United Nations and the Economic Community of Central African States

(o) Cooperation between the United Nations and the Black Sea Economic Cooperation Organization

(p) Cooperation between the United Nations and the Pacific Islands Forum

(q) Cooperation between the United Nations and the Association of Southeast Asian Nations

(r) Cooperation between the United Nations and the Community of Portuguese-speaking Countries

(s) Cooperation between the United Nations and the Shanghai Cooperation Organization

(w) Cooperation between the United Nations and the Commonwealth of Independent States

(x) Cooperation between the United Nations and the International Organization for Migration

(z) Cooperation between the United Nations and the Organisation for Economic Co-operation and Development (OECD)

Item 126. Interaction between the United Nations, national parliaments and the Inter Parliamentary Union

Item 127. Global health and foreign policy

Item 130. Sexual exploitation and abuse: implementing a zero-tolerance policy

Item 131. International cooperation on access to justice for survivors of sexual violence

Item 132. The responsibility to protect and the prevention of genocide, war crimes, ethnic cleansing and crimes against humanity

Item 133. Impact of rapid technological change on the achievement of the Sustainable Development Goals and targets

Item 134. Report of the United Nations Youth Office

Item 135. Eightieth anniversary of the end of the Second World War

Item 136. Financial reports and audited financial statements, and reports of the Board of Auditors:

(a) United Nations

(b) United Nations peacekeeping operations

(c) International Trade Centre

(d) United Nations University

(e) United Nations Development Programme

(f) United Nations Capital Development Fund

(g) United Nations Children's Fund

(h) United Nations Relief and Works Agency for Palestine Refugees in the Near East

(i) United Nations Institute for Training and Research

(j) Voluntary funds administered by the United Nations High Commissioner for Refugees

(k) Fund of the United Nations Environment Programme

(l) United Nations Population Fund

(m) United Nations Human Settlements Programme

(n) United Nations Office on Drugs and Crime

(o) United Nations Office for Project Services

(p) United Nations Entity for Gender Equality and the Empowerment of Women (UN-Women)

(q) International Residual Mechanism for Criminal Tribunals

(r) United Nations Joint Staff Pension Fund

Item 137. Review of the efficiency of the administrative and financial functioning of the United Nations

Item 138. Programme budget for 2024

Item 139. Programme budget for 2025

Item 140. Programme planning

Item 141. Improving the financial situation of the United Nations

Item 142. Pattern of conferences

Item 143. Scale of assessments for the apportionment of the expenses of the United Nations

Item 144. Human resources management

Item 145. Report on the activities of the Ethics Office

Item 146. Joint Inspection Unit

Item 147. United Nations common system

Item 148. United Nations pension system

Item 149. Administrative and budgetary coordination of the United Nations with the specialized agencies and the International Atomic Energy Agency

Item 150. Report on the activities of the Office of Internal Oversight Services

Item 151. Review of the implementation of General Assembly resolutions 48/218 B, 54/244, 59/272, 64/263, 69/253 and 74/257

Item 152. Administration of justice at the United Nations

Item 153. Financing of the International Residual Mechanism for Criminal Tribunals

Item 154. Scale of assessments for the apportionment of the expenses of United Nations peacekeeping operations

Item 155. Administrative and budgetary aspects of the financing of the United Nations peacekeeping operations

Item 156. Financing of the United Nations Interim Security Force for Abyei

Item 157. Financing of the United Nations Multidimensional Integrated Stabilization Mission in the Central African Republic

Item 158. Financing of the United Nations Peacekeeping Force in Cyprus

Item 159. Financing of the United Nations Organization Stabilization Mission in the Democratic Republic of the Congo

Item 160. Financing of the United Nations Mission in East Timor

Item 161. Financing of the United Nations Interim Administration Mission in Kosovo

Item 162. Financing of the United Nations Multidimensional Integrated Stabilization Mission in Mali

Item 163. Financing of the United Nations peacekeeping forces in the Middle East:

(a) United Nations Disengagement Observer Force

(b) United Nations Interim Force in Lebanon

Item 164. Financing of the United Nations Mission in South Sudan

Item 165. Financing of the United Nations Mission for the Referendum in Western Sahara

Item 166. Financing of the African Union-United Nations Hybrid Operation in Darfur

Item 167. Financing of the activities arising from Security Council resolution 1863 (2009)

2. *Decisions adopted on the reports of the First Committee*

79/510. Reduction of military budgets

At its 43rd plenary meeting, on 2 December 2024, the General Assembly took note of the report of the First Committee.[37]

---

[37] A/79/400.

79/511. Maintenance of international security – good-neighbourliness, stability and development in South-Eastern Europe

At its 43rd plenary meeting, on 2 December 2024, the General Assembly, on the recommendation of the First Committee,[38] decided to include in the provisional agenda of its eighty-first session the item entitled "Maintenance of international security – good-neighbourliness, stability and development in South-Eastern Europe".

79/512. Open-ended working group on the prevention of an arms race in outer space in all its aspects

At its 43rd plenary meeting, on 2 December 2024, the General Assembly, by a recorded vote of 174 to 2, with 9 abstentions,[39] on the recommendation of the First Committee,[40]

Recalling its resolution 78/20 of 4 December 2023, in which it had decided, under item 97 (d), to convene, beginning in 2025, an open-ended working group,

Recalling also its resolution 78/238 of 22 December 2023, in which it had decided, under item 97 (c), to convene, beginning in 2024, an open-ended working group,

Welcoming the consensual adoption by the Group of Governmental Experts on Further Practical Measures for the Prevention of an Arms Race in Outer Space, established pursuant to General Assembly resolution 77/250 of 30 December 2022 of its report[41] on 16 August 2024, and noting the conclusions and recommendations contained therein, including, inter alia, that that report could contribute to future work on the prevention of an arms race in outer space,

1. Decided to convene a new open-ended working group for the period 2024–2028, which would replace the two open-ended working groups established by resolutions 78/20 and 78/238;

2. Also decided to task the open-ended working group convened pursuant to paragraph 1 of the present decision to submit recommendations on the prevention of an arms race in outer space in all its aspects, and that its discussions and recommendations would be informed by all the relevant General Assembly resolutions on the prevention of an arms race in outer space, including:

(a) Resolution 78/20;

(b) Resolution 78/238;

3. Further decided:

(a) That the new open-ended working group shall work on the basis of consensus, shall hold a two-day organizational session in Geneva in 2025, and shall meet in Geneva for two substantive sessions of five days each in 2025, two substantive sessions of five days each in 2026, two substantive sessions of five days each in 2027 and two substantive sessions of five days each in 2028, with the contribution of relevant international and non-governmental organizations, and further decided that the Chair might also hold intersessional consultative meetings to exchange views on the issues within the mandate of the open-ended working group;

(b) To reaffirm that intergovernmental organizations and other entities having received a standing invitation to participate as observers in the work of the General Assembly and representatives of non-governmental organizations that were in consultative status with the Economic and Social Council, in accordance with Council resolution 1996/31 of 25 July 1996, might participate, including by speaking and submitting documents, in the formal and informal meetings of the open-ended working group as observers;

(c) That other interested non-governmental organizations relevant and competent to the scope and purpose of the open-ended working group should also inform the secretariat of their interest in participating by submitting information on the organization's purpose, programmes and activities in areas relevant to the scope of the working group; the Chair of the open-ended working group should submit the proposed list to Member States for their

[38] A/79/402, para. 7.

[39] See A/79/PV.43.

[40] A/79/406, para. 21.

[41] A/79/364.

consideration on a non-objection basis and bring the list to the attention of the working group for a final decision on participation; and those organizations would accordingly be invited to participate as observers in the formal sessions of the working group, including by speaking and submitting documents, taking into account the principles of transparency and equitable geographical representation;

4. Requested the Chair of the open-ended working group to provide an annual update to the General Assembly through its First Committee;

5. Requested the Secretary-General to provide all necessary assistance to the open-ended working group and its Chair and to transmit its report to the General Assembly at its eighty-third session, the Conference on Disarmament and the Disarmament Commission.

79/513. Treaty banning the production of fissile material for nuclear weapons or other nuclear explosive devices

At its 44th plenary meeting, on 2 December 2024, the General Assembly, by a recorded vote of 176 to 2, with 8 abstentions,[42] on the recommendation of the First Committee,[43] recalling its resolution 78/28 of 4 December 2023, decided to include in the provisional agenda of its eightieth session, under the item entitled "General and complete disarmament", the sub-item entitled "Treaty banning the production of fissile material for nuclear weapons or other nuclear explosive devices".

79/514. Missiles

At its 44th plenary meeting, on 2 December 2024, the General Assembly, by a recorded vote of 163 to 6, with 11 abstentions,[44] on the recommendation of the First Committee,[45] recalling its resolutions 54/54 F of 1 December 1999, 55/33 A of 20 November 2000, 56/24 B of 29 November 2001, 57/71 of 22 November 2002, 58/37 of 8 December 2003, 59/67 of 3 December 2004, 61/59 of 6 December 2006 and 63/55 of 2 December 2008 and its decisions 60/515 of 8 December 2005, 62/514 of 5 December 2007, 65/517 of 8 December 2010, 66/516 of 2 December 2011, 67/516 of 3 December 2012, 68/517 of 5 December 2013, 69/517 of 2 December 2014, 71/516 of 5 December 2016, 73/513 of 5 December 2018, 75/518 of 7 December 2020 and 77/515 of 7 December 2022, decided to include in the provisional agenda of its eighty-first session, under the item entitled "General and complete disarmament", the sub-item entitled "Missiles".

79/515. Compliance with non-proliferation, arms limitation and disarmament agreements and commitments

At its 44th plenary meeting, on 2 December 2024, the General Assembly, by a recorded vote of 175 to 3, with 7 abstentions,[46] on the recommendation of the First Committee,[47] recalling its resolutions 76/33 of 6 December 2021, 72/32 of 4 December 2017, 69/59 of 2 December 2014, 66/49 of 2 December 2011, 63/59 of 2 December 2008 and 60/55 of 8 December 2005, decided to include in the provisional agenda of its eightieth session, under the item entitled "General and complete disarmament", the sub-item entitled "Compliance with non-proliferation, arms limitation and disarmament agreements and commitments".

79/516. Information on requests for votes

At its 44th plenary meeting, on 2 December 2024, the General Assembly, on the recommendation of the First Committee,[48] recalling rules 87 and 127 of its rules of procedure, in which it was stated that any representative of a

[42] See A/79/PV.44.
[43] A/79/408, para. 115.
[44] See A/79/PV.44.
[45] A/79/408, para. 115.
[46] See A/79/PV.44.
[47] A/79/408, para. 115.
[48] A/79/417, para. 8.

Member State might request a recorded vote, reaffirming the need to continue to improve the working methods of the Main Committees of the Assembly, emphasizing the importance of openness, transparency and accountability in the work of the United Nations, as well as respect for the sovereign equality of all Member States, which were crucial to building trust and confidence among Member States, and recalling the invitation by the Assembly to the Chairs of the Main Committees to draw on best practices and lessons learned with a view to improving working methods:

(a) Decided that, with regard to the work of the First Committee, the identity of the Member State or States that request a vote on specific paragraphs and/or draft resolutions as a whole must be provided by the Chair of the First Committee to the Committee when requested by a Member State;

(b) Also decided to implement the decision in paragraph (a) above with immediate effect.

79/517. Provisional programme of work and timetable of the First Committee for 2025

At its 44th plenary meeting, on 2 December 2024, the General Assembly, on the recommendation of the First Committee,[49] approved the provisional programme of work and timetable of the Committee for 2025, as set out in the annex to the report of the Committee.[50]

79/518. Programme planning (First Committee)

At its 44th plenary meeting, on 2 December 2024, the General Assembly took note of the report of the First Committee.[51]

3. *Decisions adopted on the reports of the Special Political and Decolonization Committee (Fourth Committee)*

79/519. Increase in the membership of the Committee on the Peaceful Uses of Outer Space

A

At its 47th plenary meeting, on 4 December 2024, the General Assembly, on the recommendation of the Special Political and Decolonization Committee (Fourth Committee),[52] taking note of the application of Djibouti for membership in the Committee on the Peaceful Uses of Outer Space, as noted in paragraph 382 of the report of the Committee on its sixty-seventh session, held in Vienna from 19 to 28 June 2024,[53] decided to appoint Djibouti as a member of the Committee on the Peaceful Uses of Outer Space.

B

At its 47th plenary meeting, on 4 December 2024, the General Assembly, by a recorded vote of 151 to 6, with 7 abstentions,[54] on the recommendation of the Special Political and Decolonization Committee (Fourth Committee),[55] taking note of the application of Latvia for membership in the Committee on the Peaceful Uses of Outer Space, as noted in paragraph 382 of the report of the Committee on its sixty-seventh session, held in Vienna from 19 to 28 June 2024,[56] decided to appoint Latvia as a member of the Committee on the Peaceful Uses of Outer Space.

[49] A/79/417, para. 8.

[50] A/79/417.

[51] A/79/418.

[52] A/79/421, para. 19.

[53] *Official Records of the General Assembly, Seventy-ninth Session, Supplement No. 20* (A/79/20).

[54] See A/79/PV.47.

[55] A/79/421, para. 19.

[56] *Official Records of the General Assembly, Seventy-ninth Session, Supplement No. 20* (A/79/20).

79/520. Comprehensive review of the whole question of peacekeeping operations in all their aspects

At its 47th plenary meeting, on 4 December 2024, the General Assembly took note of the report of the Special Political and Decolonization Committee (Fourth Committee).[57]

79/521. Question of Gibraltar

At its 47th plenary meeting, on 4 December 2024, the General Assembly, on the recommendation of the Special Political and Decolonization Committee (Fourth Committee),[58] recalling its decision 78/513 of 7 December 2023:

(a) Urged the Governments of Spain and the United Kingdom of Great Britain and Northern Ireland, while listening to the interests and aspirations of Gibraltar that were legitimate under international law, to reach, in the spirit of the Brussels Declaration of 27 November 1984, a definitive solution to the question of Gibraltar, in the light of the relevant resolutions of the General Assembly and applicable principles, and in the spirit of the Charter of the United Nations;

(b) Took note of the desire of the United Kingdom to continue with the trilateral Forum for Dialogue;

(c) Took note of the position of Spain that the trilateral Forum for Dialogue did not exist any longer and should be replaced with a new mechanism for local cooperation in which the people of the Campo de Gibraltar and Gibraltar were represented;

(d) Welcomed the efforts made by all to resolve problems and advance in a spirit of trust and solidarity, in order to find common solutions and move forward in areas of mutual interest towards a relationship based on dialogue and cooperation.

79/522. Proposed programme of work and timetable of the Special Political and Decolonization Committee (Fourth Committee) for the eightieth session of the General Assembly

At its 47th plenary meeting, on 4 December 2024, the General Assembly, on the recommendation of the Special Political and Decolonization Committee (Fourth Committee),[59] approved the proposed programme of work and timetable of the Fourth Committee for the eightieth session of the Assembly, as set out in the report of the Committee.[60]

79/523. Programme planning (Special Political and Decolonization Committee (Fourth Committee))

At its 47th plenary meeting, on 4 December 2024, the General Assembly took note of the report of the Special Political and Decolonization Committee (Fourth Committee).[61]

4. *Decisions adopted on the reports of the Second Committee*

79/542. Macroeconomic policy questions

At its 54th plenary meeting, on 19 December 2024, the General Assembly took note of the report of the Second Committee.[62]

---

[57] A/79/424.

[58] A/79/431, para. 34.

[59] A/79/432, para. 7.

[60] A/79/432.

[61] A/79/433.

[62] A/79/435.

79/543. Groups of countries in special situations

At its 54th plenary meeting, on 19 December 2024, the General Assembly took note of the report of the Second Committee.[63]

79/544. Operational activities for development

At its 54th plenary meeting, on 19 December 2024, the General Assembly took note of the report of the Second Committee.[64]

79/545. Draft programme of work of the Second Committee for the eightieth session of the General Assembly

At its 54th plenary meeting, on 19 December 2024, the General Assembly, on the recommendation of the Second Committee:[65]

(a) Approved the draft programme of work of the Second Committee for the eightieth session of the Assembly as set out below;

(b) Invited the Bureau of the Second Committee at the eightieth session, in preparing the draft programme of work and timetable of the Committee for the eightieth session, to take into account the provisional programme of work and timetable of the Committee as contained in document A/C.2/79/CRP.1.

Draft programme of work[66]

1. Information and communications technologies for sustainable development.
2. Macroeconomic policy questions:
   (a) International trade and development;
   (b) International financial system and development;
   (c) External debt sustainability and development;
   (d) Commodities;
   (e) Financial inclusion for sustainable development;
   (f) Promotion of international cooperation to combat illicit financial flows and strengthen good practices on assets return to foster sustainable development;
   (g) Promoting investments for sustainable development;
   (h) Promotion of inclusive and effective international tax cooperation at the United Nations.
3. Follow-up to and implementation of the outcomes of the International Conferences on Financing for Development.
4. Sustainable development:
   (a) Towards the achievement of sustainable development: implementation of the 2030 Agenda for Sustainable Development, including through sustainable consumption and production, building on "Agenda 21";
   (b) Follow-up to and implementation of the Antigua and Barbuda Agenda for Small Island Developing States: A Renewed Declaration for Resilient Prosperity;

[63] A/79/440.

[64] A/79/442.

[65] A/79/446, para. 8.

[66] The final list of items and sub-items to be considered will be based on the resolutions and decisions adopted by the General Assembly.

(c) Disaster risk reduction;

(d) Protection of global climate for present and future generations of humankind;

(e) Implementation of the United Nations Convention to Combat Desertification in Those Countries Experiencing Serious Drought and/or Desertification, Particularly in Africa;

(f) Convention on Biological Diversity;

(g) Education for sustainable development;

(h) Ensuring access to affordable, reliable, sustainable and modern energy for all;

(i) Combating sand and dust storms;

(j) Sustainable mountain development;

(k) Strengthening cooperation for integrated coastal zone management for achieving sustainable development.

5. Global Code of Ethics for Tourism.

6. Globalization and interdependence:

(a) Science, technology and innovation for sustainable development;

(b) Culture and sustainable development;

(c) Development cooperation with middle-income countries.

7. Groups of countries in special situations:

(a) Follow-up to the Fifth United Nations Conference on the Least Developed Countries;

(b) Follow-up to the Third United Nations Conference on Landlocked Developing Countries.

8. Eradication of poverty and other development issues:

(a) Implementation of the Third United Nations Decade for the Eradication of Poverty (2018–2027);

(b) Eradicating rural poverty to implement the 2030 Agenda for Sustainable Development.

9. Operational activities for development:

(a) Operational activities for development of the United Nations system;

(b) South-South cooperation for development.

10. Agriculture development, food security and nutrition:

(a) Agriculture development, food security and nutrition;

(b) Natural plant fibres and sustainable development.

11. Permanent sovereignty of the Palestinian people in the Occupied Palestinian Territory, including East Jerusalem, and of the Arab population in the occupied Syrian Golan over their natural resources.

12. Revitalization of the work of the General Assembly.

13. Programme planning.

79/546. Revitalization of the work of the Second Committee

At its 54th plenary meeting, on 19 December 2024, the General Assembly, on the recommendation of the Second Committee,[67] recalling its resolution 77/335 of 1 September 2023, in particular the provisions relating to

[67] A/79/446, para. 8.

working methods, as well as its decisions 74/537 B of 11 August 2020, 75/548 B of 29 July 2021 and 77/538 B of 24 July 2023:

(a) Decided that the Bureau of the Second Committee would convene informal dialogues to discuss the revitalization of the work of the Committee in the first months of 2025;

(b) Also decided that the Second Committee would convene a plenary meeting following those dialogues to take stock of the deliberations and, as appropriate, take action on any recommendations, for subsequent approval by the General Assembly, to allow any change to come into effect ahead of the eightieth session.

79/547. Programme planning (Second Committee)

At its 54th plenary meeting, on 19 December 2024, the General Assembly took note of the report of the Second Committee.[68]

5. *Decisions adopted on the reports of the Third Committee*

79/538. Promotion and protection of human rights

At its 53rd plenary meeting, on 17 December 2024, the General Assembly took note of the report of the Third Committee.[69]

79/539. Comprehensive implementation of and follow-up to the Vienna Declaration and Programme of Action

At its 53rd plenary meeting, on 17 December 2024, the General Assembly took note of the report of the Third Committee.[70]

79/540. Draft programme of work of the Third Committee for the eightieth session of the General Assembly

At its 53rd plenary meeting, on 17 December 2024, the General Assembly, on the recommendation of the Third Committee,[71] approved, subject to any subsequent decision by the Assembly, the draft programme of work of the Third Committee for the eightieth session of the Assembly as set out below. The Assembly invited the Bureau of the Third Committee at the eightieth session, in preparing the draft programme of work and timetable of the Committee for the eightieth session, to take into account the draft provisional programme of work and timetable of the Committee, as contained in document A/C.3/79/CRP.2.

Draft programme of work

Item 1. Social development:

(a) Implementation of the outcome of the World Summit for Social Development and of the twenty-fourth special session of the General Assembly;

(b) Social development, including questions relating to the world social situation and to youth, ageing, persons with disabilities and the family.

Item 2. Crime prevention and criminal justice.

Item 3. Countering the use of information and communications technologies for criminal purposes.

---

[68] A/79/447.

[69] A/79/458.

[70] A/79/458/Add.4.

[71] A/79/462, para. 25.

Item 4. Advancement of women:

(a) Advancement of women;

(b) Implementation of the outcome of the Fourth World Conference on Women and of the twenty-third special session of the General Assembly.

Item 5. Promotion and protection of the rights of children.

Item 6. Rights of Indigenous Peoples:

(a) Rights of Indigenous Peoples;

(b) Follow-up to the outcome document of the high-level plenary meeting of the General Assembly known as the World Conference on Indigenous Peoples.

Item 7. Promotion and protection of human rights:

(a) Implementation of human rights instruments;

(b) Human rights questions, including alternative approaches for improving the effective enjoyment of human rights and fundamental freedoms;

(c) Human rights situations and reports of special rapporteurs and representatives;

(d) Comprehensive implementation of and follow-up to the Vienna Declaration and Programme of Action.

Item 8. Elimination of racism, racial discrimination, xenophobia and related intolerance:

(a) Elimination of racism, racial discrimination, xenophobia and related intolerance;

(b) Comprehensive implementation of and follow-up to the Durban Declaration and Programme of Action.

Item 9. Right of peoples to self-determination.

Item 10. Report of the Human Rights Council.

Item 11. Report of the United Nations High Commissioner for Refugees, questions relating to refugees, returnees and displaced persons and humanitarian questions.

Item 12. Revitalization of the work of the General Assembly.

Item 13. Programme planning.

79/541. Programme planning (Third Committee)

At its 53rd plenary meeting, on 17 December 2024, the General Assembly took note of the report of the Third Committee.[72]

6. *Decisions adopted on the reports of the Fifth Committee*

79/549. Administrative and budgetary coordination of the United Nations with the specialized agencies and the International Atomic Energy Agency

At its 55th (resumed) plenary meeting, on 24 December 2024, the General Assembly took note of the report of the Fifth Committee.[73]

[72] A/79/463.

[73] A/79/647.

79/550. Report on the activities of the Office of Internal Oversight Services

At its 55th (resumed) plenary meeting, on 24 December 2024, the General Assembly took note of the report of the Fifth Committee.[74]

79/551. Questions deferred for future consideration

At its 55th (resumed) plenary meeting, on 24 December 2024, the General Assembly, on the recommendation of the Fifth Committee,[75]

Section A

Decided to defer until the first part of its resumed seventy-ninth session consideration of the following documents:

Item 139

Proposed programme budget for 2025

Information and communications technology strategy

Report of the Secretary-General on the refined elements of the information and communications technology strategy[76]

Related report of the Advisory Committee on Administrative and Budgetary Questions[77]

Item 150

Report on the activities of the Office of Internal Oversight Services

Report of the Office of Internal Oversight Services on the activities of the Office for the period from 1 July 2023 to 30 June 2024[78]

Report of the Independent Audit Advisory Committee on its activities for the period from 1 August 2023 to 31 July 2024[79]

Section B

Decided to defer until the main part of its eightieth session consideration of the following documents:

Item 139

Proposed programme budget for 2025

Estimates in respect of special political missions

Report of the Secretary-General on the review of arrangements for funding and backstopping special political missions[80]

Related report of the Advisory Committee on Administrative and Budgetary Questions[81]

---

[74] A/79/648.

[75] A/79/653, para. 9.

[76] A/79/339.

[77] A/79/7/Add.17.

[78] A/79/309 (Part I) and A/79/309 (Part I)/Add.1.

[79] A/79/310.

[80] A/66/340.

[81] A/66/7/Add.21.

7. *Decisions adopted on the reports of the Sixth Committee*

79/524. Provisional programme of work of the Sixth Committee for the eightieth session

At its 47th plenary meeting, on 4 December 2024, the General Assembly, on the recommendation of the Sixth Committee,[82] noted that the Committee had decided to adopt the following provisional programme of work for the eightieth session of the Assembly, as proposed by the Bureau:

Provisional programme of work[83]

6 October	Organization of work of the Sixth Committee
	Revitalization of the work of the General Assembly
6 and 7 October	Measures to eliminate international terrorism
8 October	Programme planning
8 and 9 October	The rule of law at the national and international levels
9 and 10 October	Criminal accountability of United Nations officials and experts on mission
10 and 13 October	Responsibility of States for internationally wrongful acts
13 and 14 October	Crimes against humanity
14 October	Protection of persons in the event of disasters
15 October	Request(s) for observer status[84]
	Strengthening and promoting the international treaty framework
16 October	Report of the Special Committee on the Charter of the United Nations and on the Strengthening of the Role of the Organization
20 and 21 October	Report of the United Nations Commission on International Trade Law on the work of its fifty-eighth session
21 October	Administration of justice at the United Nations
21 and 22 October	The scope and application of the principle of universal jurisdiction
23 October	Diplomatic protection
	United Nations Programme of Assistance in the Teaching, Study, Dissemination and Wider Appreciation of International Law
27 to 31 October and 4 to 6 November	Report of the International Law Commission on the work of its seventy-sixth session
7 November	Report of the Committee on Relations with the Host Country
14 November	Request(s) for observer status[85]
	Revitalization of the work of the General Assembly (*continued*)
21 November	Election of the officers of the Main Committees
24 October and 10 November	Reserved

[82] A/79/491, para. 6.

[83] Indicating provisional dates in 2025 for debates under the respective items without prejudice to the allocation of additional meetings for working groups established and Secretariat briefings convened by the Sixth Committee.

[84] Request(s) for observer status included, for the first time, in the agenda of the eightieth session.

[85] Request(s) for observer status deferred from previous sessions.

79/525. Programme planning (Sixth Committee)

At its 47th plenary meeting, on 4 December 2024, the General Assembly took note of the report of the Sixth Committee.[86]

79/526. Observer status for the Cooperation Council of Turkic-speaking States in the General Assembly

At its 47th plenary meeting, on 4 December 2024, the General Assembly, on the recommendation of the Sixth Committee,[87] decided to defer a decision on the request for observer status for the Cooperation Council of Turkic-speaking States in the Assembly[88] until the eightieth session of the Assembly.

79/527. Observer status for the Eurasian Economic Union in the General Assembly

At its 47th plenary meeting, on 4 December 2024, the General Assembly, on the recommendation of the Sixth Committee,[89] decided to defer a decision on the request for observer status for the Eurasian Economic Union in the Assembly[90] until the eightieth session of the Assembly.

79/528. Observer status for the Community of Democracies in the General Assembly

At its 47th plenary meeting, on 4 December 2024, the General Assembly, on the recommendation of the Sixth Committee,[91] decided to defer a decision on the request for observer status for the Community of Democracies in the Assembly[92] until the eightieth session of the Assembly.

79/529. Observer status for the Ramsar Convention on Wetlands Secretariat in the General Assembly

At its 47th plenary meeting, on 4 December 2024, the General Assembly, on the recommendation of the Sixth Committee,[93] decided to defer a decision on the request for observer status for the Ramsar Convention on Wetlands Secretariat in the Assembly[94] until the eightieth session of the Assembly.

79/530. Observer status for the Global Environment Facility in the General Assembly

At its 47th plenary meeting, on 4 December 2024, the General Assembly, on the recommendation of the Sixth Committee,[95] decided to defer a decision on the request for observer status for the Global Environment Facility in the Assembly[96] until the eightieth session of the Assembly.

79/531. Observer status for the International Organization of Employers in the General Assembly

At its 47th plenary meeting, on 4 December 2024, the General Assembly, on the recommendation of the Sixth Committee,[97] decided to defer a decision on the request for observer status for the International Organization of Employers in the Assembly[98] until the eightieth session of the Assembly.

---

[86] A/79/492.

[87] A/79/480, para. 7.

[88] See A/66/141.

[89] A/79/481, para. 7.

[90] See A/70/141.

[91] A/79/482, para. 7.

[92] See A/70/142.

[93] A/79/483, para. 7.

[94] See A/72/194.

[95] A/79/484, para. 7.

[96] See A/72/195.

[97] A/79/485, para. 7.

[98] See A/74/291.

79/532. Observer status for the International Trade Union Confederation in the General Assembly

At its 47th plenary meeting, on 4 December 2024, the General Assembly, on the recommendation of the Sixth Committee,[99] decided to defer a decision on the request for observer status for the International Trade Union Confederation in the Assembly[100] until the eightieth session of the Assembly.

79/533. Observer status for the Boao Forum for Asia in the General Assembly

At its 47th plenary meeting, on 4 December 2024, the General Assembly, on the recommendation of the Sixth Committee,[101] decided to defer a decision on the request for observer status for the Boao Forum for Asia in the Assembly[102] until the eightieth session of the Assembly.

79/534. Observer status for the International Parliamentarians' Congress in the General Assembly

At its 47th plenary meeting, on 4 December 2024, the General Assembly, on the recommendation of the Sixth Committee,[103] decided to defer a decision on the request for observer status for the International Parliamentarians' Congress in the General Assembly[104] until the eightieth session of the Assembly.

79/535. Observer status for the Regional Anti-Corruption Initiative in the General Assembly

At its 47th plenary meeting, on 4 December 2024, the General Assembly, on the recommendation of the Sixth Committee,[105] decided to defer a decision on the request for observer status for the Regional Anti-Corruption Initiative in the Assembly[106] until the eightieth session of the Assembly.

[99] A/79/486, para. 7.

[100] See A/74/292.

[101] A/79/487, para. 7.

[102] See A/74/293.

[103] A/79/488, para. 7.

[104] See A/78/141.

[105] A/79/489, para. 8.

[106] See A/79/141.

Annex

Checklist of decisions

Decision number	*Title*	*Item*	*Plenary meeting*	*Date of adoption*	*Page*
79/401.	Appointment of the members of the Credentials Committee	3 (a)	1st	10 September 2024	4
79/402.	Extension of the appointment of the Under-Secretary-General for Internal Oversight Services	116 (j)	2nd	13 September 2024	4
79/403.	Election of members of the Human Rights Council	115 (c)	19th	9 October 2024	4
79/404.	Election of members of the Committee for Programme and Coordination	115 (a)	38th	13 November 2024	4
79/405.	Election of members of the Permanent Forum of People of African Descent	115 (e)	38th	13 November 2024	5
79/406.	Appointment of members of the Committee on Conferences	116 (f)	38th	13 November 2024	5
79/407.	Appointment of members of the Advisory Committee on Administrative and Budgetary Questions	116 (a)	38th	13 November 2024	5
79/408.	Appointment of members of the Committee on Contributions	116 (b)	38th	13 November 2024	6
79/409.	Confirmation of the appointment of members of the Investments Committee	116 (c)	38th	13 November 2024	6
79/410.	Appointment of members of the International Civil Service Commission	116 (d)	38th	13 November 2024	6
79/411.	Appointment of members and alternate members of the United Nations Staff Pension Committee	116 (e)	38th 48th	13 November 2024 6 December 2024	7
79/412.	Election of members of the United Nations Commission on International Trade Law	115 (d)	40th	20 November 2024	7
79/413.	Election of members of the Organizational Committee of the Peacebuilding Commission	115 (b)	54th	19 December 2024	8
79/501.	Meetings of subsidiary organs and entities during the main part of the seventy-ninth session	7	1st	10 September 2024	9
79/502.	General debate of the seventy-ninth session of the General Assembly	7	2nd	13 September 2024	9
79/503.	Rights of reply to addresses by Heads of State	7	2nd	13 September 2024	9
79/504.	Organization of the seventy-ninth session	7	2nd 42nd 52nd	13 September 2024 26 November 2024 12 December 2024	9
79/505.	Adoption of the agenda and allocation of agenda items	7	2nd 54th	13 September 2024 19 December 2024	10
79/506.	Summit of the Future				
	Decision A	123	3rd	22 September 2024	10
	Decision B	123	3rd	22 September 2024	10
79/507.	Report of the International Residual Mechanism for Criminal Tribunals	128	23rd	16 October 2024	11
79/508.	Report of the International Court of Justice	73	31st	30 October 2024	11

79/509.	Report of the Economic and Social Council	9	34th	5 November 2024	11
79/510.	Reduction of military budgets	90	43rd	2 December 2024	24
79/511.	Maintenance of international security – good-neighbourliness, stability and development in South-Eastern Europe	92	43rd	2 December 2024	25
79/512.	Open-ended working group on the prevention of an arms race in outer space in all its aspects	96 (a)	43rd	2 December 2024	25
79/513.	Treaty banning the production of fissile material for nuclear weapons or other nuclear explosive devices	98 (a)	44th	2 December 2024	26
79/514.	Missiles	98 (s)	44th	2 December 2024	26
79/515.	Compliance with non-proliferation, arms limitation and disarmament agreements and commitments	98 (ee)	44th	2 December 2024	26
79/516.	Information on requests for votes	121	44th	2 December 2024	26
79/517.	Provisional programme of work and timetable of the First Committee for 2025	121	44th	2 December 2024	27
79/518.	Programme planning (First Committee)	140	44th	2 December 2024	27
79/519.	Increase in the membership of the Committee on the Peaceful Uses of Outer Space				
	Decision A	48	47th	4 December 2024	27
	Decision B	48	47th	4 December 2024	27
79/520.	Comprehensive review of the whole question of peacekeeping operations in all their aspects	51	47th	4 December 2024	28
79/521.	Question of Gibraltar	58	47th	4 December 2024	28
79/522.	Proposed programme of work and timetable of the Special Political and Decolonization Committee (Fourth Committee) for the eightieth session of the General Assembly	121	47th	4 December 2024	28
79/523.	Programme planning (Special Political and Decolonization Committee (Fourth Committee))	140	47th	4 December 2024	28
79/524.	Provisional programme of work of the Sixth Committee for the eightieth session	121	47th	4 December 2024	34
79/525.	Programme planning (Sixth Committee)	140	47th	4 December 2024	35
79/526.	Observer status for the Cooperation Council of Turkic-speaking States in the General Assembly	169	47th	4 December 2024	35
79/527.	Observer status for the Eurasian Economic Union in the General Assembly	170	47th	4 December 2024	35
79/528.	Observer status for the Community of Democracies in the General Assembly	171	47th	4 December 2024	35
79/529.	Observer status for the Ramsar Convention on Wetlands Secretariat in the General Assembly	172	47th	4 December 2024	35
79/530.	Observer status for the Global Environment Facility in the General Assembly	173	47th	4 December 2024	35
79/531.	Observer status for the International Organization of Employers in the General Assembly	174	47th	4 December 2024	35

79/532.	Observer status for the International Trade Union Confederation in the General Assembly	175	47th	4 December 2024	36
79/533.	Observer status for the Boao Forum for Asia in the General Assembly	176	47th	4 December 2024	36
79/534.	Observer status for the International Parliamentarians' Congress in the General Assembly	177	47th	4 December 2024	36
79/535.	Observer status for the Regional Anti-Corruption Initiative in the General Assembly	178	47th	4 December 2024	36
79/536.	Report of the Credentials Committee	3 (b)	48th	6 December 2024	11
79/537.	Further modalities of the Third United Nations Conference on Landlocked Developing Countries				
	Decision A	13	48th	6 December 2024	11
	Decision B	13	55th (resumed)	24 December 2024	12
	Decision C	13	55th (resumed)	24 December 2024	12
79/538.	Promotion and protection of human rights	71	53rd	17 December 2024	31
79/539.	Comprehensive implementation of and follow-up to the Vienna Declaration and Programme of Action	71 (d)	53rd	17 December 2024	31
79/540.	Draft programme of work of the Third Committee for the eightieth session of the General Assembly	121	53rd	17 December 2024	31
79/541.	Programme planning (Third Committee)	140	53rd	17 December 2024	32
79/542.	Macroeconomic policy questions	16	54th	19 December 2024	28
79/543.	Groups of countries in special situations	21	54th	19 December 2024	29
79/544.	Operational activities for development	23	54th	19 December 2024	29
79/545.	Draft programme of work of the Second Committee for the eightieth session of the General Assembly	121	54th	19 December 2024	29
79/546.	Revitalization of the work of the Second Committee	121	54th	19 December 2024	30
79/547.	Programme planning (Second Committee)	140	54th	19 December 2024	31
79/548.	Participation of non-governmental organizations, civil society organizations, academic institutions and the private sector in the Fourth International Conference on Financing for Development	17	54th	19 December 2024	12
79/549.	Administrative and budgetary coordination of the United Nations with the specialized agencies and the International Atomic Energy Agency	149	55th (resumed)	24 December 2024	32
79/550.	Report on the activities of the Office of Internal Oversight Services	137 and 150	55th (resumed)	24 December 2024	33
79/551.	Questions deferred for future consideration	137	55th (resumed)	24 December 2024	33
79/552.	Agenda items remaining for consideration by the General Assembly at its seventy-ninth session	7	55th (resumed)	24 December 2024	20